Copyright © 2022 by Laura Goodsell

All rights reserved.

This book or any portion thereof may not be reproduced or used in any manner whatsoever without the express written permission of the publisher except for the use of brief quotations in a book review.

First Printing, 2022
ISBN 9798840673713

# Well Hello...

You've bought this amazing book! Thank you so much, I really hope you like it, a lot of hard work and dedication has gone into the contents of this book, contributed to by many wonderful small business owners, none of whom are professional graphic designers, which says a lot as the quality of the graphics in here are amazing!

So... What will you discover here today? Well that's up to you, would you like to learn more about all of the small businesses here? Or discover how these graphics have been created? Or use them as inspiration for your own designs? Yep, you can find it all right here.

You may be wondering who I am as well? Who is this person that created this book, connecting so many wonderful people?

Well that would be me. Hi, I'm Laura, I'm an award winning small business owner myself, Canva Design Coach and a Canva Creator Ambassador for the UK - we're called Canvassadors!
I love helping other small business owners with their graphics, branding, creating passive income through template and element creation, or setting up a new digital design business. Anything design related and I'm there.

Encouraging women to embrace design and create businesses within the digital world is one of my all time passions.

I've built my business around my family life, I have two boys, Oliver and Alfie, plus two Labrador puppies, - so life is never dull and I live in the middle of the UK.

After pivoting my business at the start of lockdown (I'm a web designer) I decided to focus my attention on helping businesses become more visible on social media, I have a business full of design based services, such as my monthly Canva template membership (full of template packs and tutorial videos), Canva courses for all levels, challenges, trainings into business groups and creating templates for the Canva library.

Then there is this awesome book project, aimed at helping businesses with visibility, showcasing their Canva designs, and to give you a physical reference book for your own design inspiration.

**This is just the beginning of an exciting journey.**
www.businessdesignacademy.co.uk

Laura x

# Anna Rump

**Name:**

Anna Rump

**Business:**

Amelia Rose Media Ltd

### Who do you help with your business?

I help stressed, overwhelmed and time poor business owners to have a profitable and stress free social media presence.

### What products or services do you offer?

I offer content creation, lead generation, community management, full platform management and platform audits, as well as strategy creation.

### How long have you been using Canva and what do you create?

I have been using Canva for about a year now and make graphics for both my own profiles and for my clients. I am going to be branching out to make more things now as this challenge has really inspired me!

### What advice would you offer someone just starting out?

Follow your instincts, don't be afraid to ask for help, and learn to accept rejection as it's not personal.

### What or who in the world inspires you?

My daughter, Eloise, is a daily inspiration. When you can see how a three year old views the world it suddenly becomes a place full of wonder and adventure.

### How did you create this piece?

I decided I wanted something peaceful and grounded in nature and so I started with the background. After that I chose various watercolour elements and layered them into place, changing the angles of some and the rotation of others.

### How can we contact you?

 @annarump    @the.social.media.lady    www.ameliarosemedia.net

# Stephanie Wium

### Name:

Stephanie Wium

### Business:

Simply On Demand - Creative Designer and Canva Design Coach

### Who do you help with your business?

I am a Canva Design Coach helping VAs & SMMs design better and be more confident with 1:1 design coaching. Helping coaches show up visually visible in their own business with designs created for them.

### What products or services do you offer?

Canva design coaching
Creative design services

### How long have you been using Canva and what do you create?

For almost three years now, I started out using it only for myself, but have developed my whole business model around this versatile online drag and drop tool.

### What advice would you offer someone just starting out?

Don't be scared to try. Just start, once started you can course adjust. None of us started out as experts in any of our fields. Be prepared to learn along the way. Austin Kleon says in his book, Steal Like an Artist "Don't wait until you know who you are to get started. Just dive in head first and start doing! It's the best way to learn and you can only grow!"

### What or who in the world inspires you?

My kids moved to a new country where they had NO support. If they can do it, so can I. They are my inspiration to always look at the unknown as an adventure, an opportunity to learn and to grow.

---

### How did you create this piece?

Elements used from within Canva. Shadows applied to create realistic lighting effect. Painting overlaid with a grid to insert a typical New Zealand Hobbit home door used from within Canva photos. Wall background faded to create depth.

### How can we contact you?

 www.simplyondemand.net

 @simplyondemand     stephanie_wium     @StephanieWium

# Paula Garrard

**Name:**

Paula Garrard

**Business:**

By Paula Photography

### Who do you help with your business?

Ambitious business owners that want to grow and need awesome photographs for marketing purposes.

### What products or services do you offer?

Brand photography for small business owners that really want to stand out online.

### How long have you been using Canva and what do you create?

About three years. I use it mainly for social media graphics for my business but also enjoy creating images for pleasure.

### What advice would you offer someone just starting out?

Play around with templates. See how they are put together and just have fun experimenting. You don't have to get it right first time!

### What or who in the world inspires you?

I'm inspired by people that achieve their dreams through sheer guts and determination even in the face of adversity. I admire those that demonstrate both resilience and vulnerability

---

### How did you create this piece?

My design is made up of lots of individual elements combined together in layers. I started with the mountains and added rectangles in matching colours using the colour picker tool for the sky and grass. Then I added all the different elements to create the final image.

### How can we contact you?

 @bypaulag      @bypaulagarrard

# Tracy Richardson

CREATIVE DESIGN PROJECT

**Name:**

Tracy Richardson

**Business:**

Hybrid Therapy

## Who do you help with your business?

I help busy health conscious individuals looking to reduce pain, renew energy and restore wellness. Because, being well creates the freedom to live life the way you want.

## What products or services do you offer?

I offer one to one therapy, coaching, workshops and guest speaking for private and corporate groups and training for wellness pros. I'm also the host of the Simply Mindful Wellness podcast, and an author with my new book The Little Book of Wellness to be published shortly.

## How long have you been using Canva and what do you create?

I've been using Canva since 2017, I use it to create social media graphics, lead magnets, presentation slides, pdf documents... basically anything that needs a little colour or artistic flair.

## What advice would you offer someone just starting out?

Just try things - give them a go and see what works for you. There are lots of people like Laura, who are able to give you advice, but like anything new it's about trying it and seeing if it works for you.

## What or who in the world inspires you?

I'm inspired every day by the sun shining through the window as each day is a new opportunity for an adventure!

---

## How did you create this piece?

Using elements, images, image editing and wanting to create something that represents the soulful and spiritual side of me.

## How can we contact you?

   @hybridtherapy.uk    www.hybridtherapy.uk

CREATIVE DESIGN PROJECT

# Mina Ahmed

CREATIVE DESIGN PROJECT

## Name:

Mina Ahmed

## Business:

Psychotherapist

## Who do you help with your business?

Therapy, Therapeutic and Emotional Support for Ambitious Women with Stress, Anxiety and Trauma Challenges.

## What products or services do you offer?

Brain Working Recursive Therapy (BWRT), Certified Master Life Coaching Neuro-Linguistic Programming (NLP)

## How long have you been using Canva and what do you create?

Fairly new to Canva although, last year I used it to explore creating something for my face book and website main images. I have now used Canva and created a piece of artwork for a book page within the book.

## What advice would you offer someone just starting out?

Canva has some very interesting and creative ideas to produce graphics that can be used in business and workshop advertising. I found the tools simple to access and easy to insert and manipulate. It is good fun and I would encourage people to start using this product and develop further advanced skills so they could use these to produce marketing or other materials.

## What or who in the world inspires you?

I am inspired by Daniel Goleman an author, psychologist and science journalist who discusses brain architecture and concepts around self awareness. Ideas and concepts that I also use with my clients in the field of mind health for Anxiety, Stress and Trauma processing.

---

## How did you create this piece?

I started by thinking of a theme that inspired me, which is nature, I thought about looking outside of a window frame because working from home is something many of us have to do since the pandemic. So I imagined what I would like to look at if I looked outside my window during my short breaks. I first chose a background colour of purple and then selected a gold arch design from the graphics and was inspired to use plants and flowers around this, almost as if they were hanging off this arch. I then selected a range of flowers and plant images to add around this arch and searched for flower borders that could fill some of the spaces around the far corners of the image. Whilst searching I came across an image that looked like a sun, choosing a circular band of flowers and shaping it so that it looked like a moon crescent shape and placed it inside the sun image. Once all plants and flowers were selected I moved these images around the background shape and when I was happy with the setting I added a square gold frame to represent the window frame. Then I moved some of the images either in front or behind the frame by using the move-to function. This function allowed the window to appear as if it could be inside a room view or from an outside view of someone looking at a window on a house.

## How can we contact you?

 @mindpeace.uk     @mindpeace.uk     https://www.mindpeace.uk/

## Jessica Weeks

CREATIVE DESIGN PROJECT

**Name:**

Jessica Weeks

**Business:**

Hannah's House

## Who do you help with your business?

Hannah's House was born after the death of our daughter Emelia, in 2017. We are a bereavement charity that provides support for children after the death of a sibling through any kind of babyloss. We help bereaved parents support their children and have hope after loss. Coming alongside the whole family for every step of the journey through to healing after babyloss.

## What products or services do you offer?

We support families through peer-to-peer befriending, a parenting after loss group and pregnancy after loss support where we provide maternity clothes, amongst other things. We also provide sibling support bags to children who have lost a brother or sister to babyloss. Our Annual Event "Emelia's Birthday Party" is an opportunity in the midst of the gloom of January to get dressed up in your best party outfit, donate to Hannah's House and share a picture on social media using one of our #'s, #emeliasbirthdayparty #hannahshousecov #teamemelia. The money raised enables us to continue helping the families we support through the Parenting with Hope Group (parenting after loss group) supporting mums through pregnancy after loss and training our staff in the Grief Recovery Method.

## How long have you been using Canva and what do you create?

I've been using Canva since 2018, I create social media posts and stories for the charity (we have Facebook, Instagram and LinkedIn accounts). I also create postcards for our groups, business cards and information flyers, I like the flexibility of the pro account, which is free for charities and non-profits.

## What advice would you offer someone just starting out?

Don't wait for everything to be perfect before you start, sometimes you just need to share what you have and build from there. Always remember why you started, there will be days where your motivation has evaporated that's where discipline and your "why" take over to push you forward.

## What or who in the world inspires you?

Shortly after Emelia died I became really embarrassed to talk about her, I imagined that people were thinking "she's talking about her dead baby again!..." they weren't, the stigma was all in my head. Then I was reminded of the bible verse I prayed every day of my pregnancy... "I shall not die, but live and declare the works of the Lord" – Psalms 118:17. I now take every opportunity to tell her story, because her story will become a page in another family's survival guide.

## How did you create this piece?

I thought about the hope that I want Hannah's House to bring to bereaved families, the things that we found helpful after Emelia's death and the waves of changing emotions that we experienced. I want families experiencing babyloss to know that despite all of the pain that they have experienced hope can be found on the journey to healing. I have portrayed this through all of the black and dark grey images in the background showing what has been lost, which gives way to bright hope at the foreground of the piece. Emelia Isabelle Weeks, you shall live and not die – forever my girl.

## How can we contact you?

 @hannahshousecov   hannahshousecov  www.hannahshouse.org.uk

CREATIVE DESIGN PROJECT

# Sharon Barry

CREATIVE DESIGN PROJECT

**Name:**

Sharon Barry

**Business:**

Little Gem Virtual Business Services

### Who do you help with your business?

I work with busy entrepreneurs and small business owners who don't have the time, knowledge, resources or desire to do the essential admin and tech tasks for their business.

### What products or services do you offer?

I offer a wide variety of business administration services including website maintenance and management, social media services, creating graphics for blogs, websites and social media.

### How long have you been using Canva and what do you create?

I have been using Canva for four years. I initially started using Canva to create images to use on my social media posts and have in recent months created covers for a range of self-published notebooks. I also create social media/blog post images for my clients as well.

### What advice would you offer someone just starting out?

Have fun with Canva, play around with it and find out what it can do. You don't need a Pro version to get great results from Canva, I've used the free version for the past four years and always manage to create what I need and never feel as though I'm missing out by not upgrading. If you feel you need the more premium features on a regular basis, then it's worth the investment.

### What or who in the world inspires you?

I've always been a fan of fantasy and sci-fi genres and I love to create images that are a little bit different from everything else out there. I'll take a template image and will create something unique and stunning from an image that started out looking fairly run of the mill or ordinary.
There is no end to the magic you can create, it's a wonderful place to let your imagination run free.

---

### How did you create this piece?

I searched for a watercolour background and picked a design and colour that stood out for me.
I love mandalas and wanted to see what I could use that would work with my background from the elements section. To make sure I had every Canva feature at my disposal, I did opt for the free 30-day pro trial and chose a mixture of designs from the free and premium range.

### How can we contact you?

 @littlegemva     @littlegem.va     www.littlegemva.com

CREATIVE DESIGN PROJECT

# Naomi Jane Johnson

## Name:

Naomi Jane Johnson

## Business:

Digital Content Designer

## Who do you help with your business?

Coaches, therapists and course creators who want to stand out from their competitors with innovative products and ideas that don't require degree-level design skills.

## What products or services do you offer?

Journal and planner design - done for you or taught via an online course. A range of digital / online products such as printables, digital business cards, promotional videos, masterclasses.

## How long have you been using Canva and what do you create?

I joined Canva in 2013 - I use it every day to create graphics and videos for social media and my websites, also for journal/planner design, and as a Canva Creator I produce templates.

## What advice would you offer someone just starting out?

Spend time exploring all the tools and menus - try editing a few templates to begin with. Take a look at the Canva blog and the many tutorials provided for further inspiration and ideas.

## What or who in the world inspires you?

Other designers, blogs and articles I come across, tutorials and ideas via YouTube and other social media, world events, the beauty of nature.

---

## How did you create this piece?

I started with the tiger head photo, removed the background, added various effects. Then I used various "alcohol ink" elements with effects such as Glow, Photogenic, Slice and Liquify, duplicated and overlaid several on top of each other.

## How can we contact you?

 hello@naomijanejohnson.co.uk

 @createwithnaomi     @naomijanejohnson     www.naomijanejohnson.co.uk

# Laura Goodsell

## Name:

Laura Goodsell

## Business:

Canva Coach and Digital designer at The Business Design Academy

## Who do you help with your business?

I'm a Canva Creator Ambassador for the UK and I help all small businesses who would love to learn more about Canva and how it could work for their business, from creating social graphics, branding and semi-passive income through template and element design.

## What products or services do you offer?

I run courses, all based on Canva, from Canva beginners, to more advanced passive income set up's, branding and template packs. I also run trainings into business groups, create templates for the Canva library, run a template membership and create a yearly business planner, notebooks and of course this amazing book you are holding right now.

## How long have you been using Canva and what do you create?

I've been using Canva almost daily since 2017, I love everything about the ease of use and simplicity, but you can still create amazing designs. I mainly create social media templates, but I love to create client ebooks and planners as well, as it lets me delve deeper into the design process.

## What advice would you offer someone just starting out?

Open a blank template and press all the buttons, really get to know what everything does, don't be afraid, you can just delete the design if all goes wrong, plus check out YouTube for inspirational ideas.

## What or who in the world inspires you?

So many other designers inspire me daily, I love to learn and see what new trends are out there. Plus my children, I have two boys and I want to show them that you can achieve anything if you have the passion and determination - you can succeed.

---

## How did you create this piece?

This was started with a blank template and I searched "watercolour" as the keyword, I used only watercolour elements and placed them to create the design, then I used "shadow" and added some shadow elements along the bottom to give the look of a deep dark forest but the top is light and full of life.

## How can we contact you?

  @createoncanva      laura@businessdesignacademy.co.uk

  @createoncanvawithlaura      www.businessdesignacademy.co.uk

CREATIVE DESIGN PROJECT

**Joanna Cates**

20          CREATIVE DESIGN PROJECT

**Name:**

Joanna Cates

**Business:**

The Visual Storyteller, Joanna Cates Creates.

## Who do you help with your business?

I teach midlife businesswomen how to create short content videos, Canva creations, and be able to take unique photographs that will help them stand out from the competition.

## What products or services do you offer?

Step-by-step training with evergreen courses, one to one support, or bite size learning in Joanna Cates Creates Academy.

## How long have you been using Canva and what do you create?

I am also a self-published author of midlife romance, so as The Saucy Author, I turned to Canva to create all my social media marketing content. For Joanna Cates Creates, I use Canva for training purposes as well as marketing. I have been using Canva for several years, as I started out creating slideshows and invitations for personal us, before using it for business purposes.

## What advice would you offer someone just starting out?

To quote Donald Miller, 'clarify your messages so your customers will listen.' This also applies to visual content. Try not to add too much text to an image or short video, as you only have a short window of time to capture your viewers attention. Marketing trends are leaning towards short-content video as they are more engaging. Therefore, if you don't already know how to, learn the skills to create eye-catching videos.

## What or who in the world inspires you?

Whilst studying photography, I was inspired by American born Jerry Uelsmann, the master of photomontage, and Catherine McIntyre, a computer artist living in Scotland. Both artists create surreal images made up of layers, and this inspired me to create my own works of art using Photoshop. As Canva designs are made up of layers, they can be credited as a source of inspiration for my business.

## How did you create this piece?

Firstly, I created a blank design with custom sizes. I selected three of my own black and white stock photographs and uploaded them to Canva. I selected a Grid suitable for three images and added them to the sections, adjusting the spacing. Using Canva editing tools, I blurred one image (Leaning Tower of Pisa) and added a filter to the giraffe to match the black and white tones. I also added a highlight to the giraffe's eye, using shapes. The next step was to add a rectangle shape to act as a text box. The transparency was adjusted to allow for the images to be visible and I adjusted the colour to pink, to match my brand colours. For the lettering, I used frames and spelled out the words 'Black and White.' Once happy with the alignment, I grouped them to resize them to fit the design. I selected black and white photographs from Canva's stock images and added them to each individual frame.

## How can we contact you?

 @joannacatescreates     @joannacatescreates     www.joannacatescreates.co.uk

# Natalie McCoy

CREATIVE DESIGN PROJECT

### Name:

Natalie McCoy

### Business:

Urban Soul Holistic Therapy

### Who do you help with your business?

I help and support individuals that may be suffering with their health and well-being either mentally or physically. I offer a tailored service to each and every client concentrating on their needs and putting a treatment plan together for them.

### What products or services do you offer?

I offer a range of holistic treatments to support people's health and well-being. This could be from clients suffering from anxiety through to those suffering from a sports injury. These treatments include various massages, reflexology, Indian head massage, pregnancy massage, skin care treatments and procedures and also Gentle Release Therapy. I also offer well-being talks to the wider community as well.

### How long have you been using Canva and what do you create?

I have been using free canva on and off for the four years that I have been in business but invested this year in the Pro side of it to be able to produce better images and to be able to use this set-up more for my social media and the content that I need to keep people engaged. I have found using the pro version that you can do more advanced things and end up with a greater and better image.

### What advice would you offer someone just starting out?

When starting out invest in what you need as this will reduce the outlay of time that you have to do things in the future for example Canva pro, QuickBooks or Zero, networking, and remembering that you are not on your own.

### What or who in the world inspires you?

My little boy inspires me every day to be the best role model I can be for him and to inspire to push myself to achieve my dream not only for myself but also for our family.

---

### How did you create this piece?

When I started this image I came up with a concept first and then worked through the Canva steps. Firstly, I looked at a background that could bring my image to life, the next step was looking for clouds to go with the image and then looking for the wording and accessorising the other pictures with the wording.

### How can we contact you?

urbansoulholistictherapy

# Jillian Horan

## Name:

Jillian Horan

## Business:

I run two businesses - Heavenly Skincare and Cosmetics as well as my Virtual Assistant business JillH VA.

## Who do you help with your business?

I help ladies primarily (but men also) to find solutions to any skincare concerns or issues they may have, thus helping them gain confidence.

My VA business helps small business owners, retail, health & wellness and beauty based businesses.

## What products or services do you offer?

Skincare and cosmetics with one to one consultations, offering clear advice and using natural ethical products with samples to try.

In my VA role I offer social media templates and graphics as well as virtual assistance to small business owners with admin tasks, social media strategy, email marketing and more.

## How long have you been using Canva and what do you create?

I have used Canva for around two years. I do use it mostly for social media, but also ebooks, presentations, certificates for team members, flyers, calendars and recently a website.

## What advice would you offer someone just starting out?

Always trust in yourself. Don't overthink and talk yourself out of a perfectly good idea. Absolute perfection probably does not exist!

## What or who in the world inspires you?

My son and grandchildren as they have overcome so much and are excelling in life.

---

## How did you create this piece?

I was drawn to create something fairytale as I do so love this genre. I selected watercolour elements with a fairytale theme. I layered background watercolour elements, adjusting transparency till it looked nicely muted. Then I placed chosen elements in layers, behind and in front accordingly. I wanted to keep it a simple and uncluttered design.

## How can we contact you?

**Heavenly Skincare and Cosmetics:**

 @heavenlyskincareandcosmeticsuk   @heavenlyskincareandcosmetics

**Virtual Assistant business JillH VA:**

 @JillHVirtualAssistant   @jillh_va

**Jemma Stevens**

### Name:
Jemma Stevens

### Business:
Flawsome Jem, CBD Products, Education & Support

### Who do you help with your business?
I motivate, inspire, educate and empower you in all things CBD, health, wellbeing and meditation, so you can live your best life forever!

### What products or services do you offer?
I offer a large affordable range of award winning, lab tested, FSA approved CBD Products, including; Tinctures/Drops, Gummies, Tabz, Topicals and Bath Bombs.

### How long have you been using Canva and what do you create?
I have been using Canva for about three years now. I use it to create social media graphics and posts. I also use it for creating resources for my business, e.g. workbooks, recipe books, guides, planners and trackers. I have created and self published a book on Amazon that I created on canva too! Love me a bit of Canva!

### What advice would you offer someone just starting out?
I am a complete tech phobe so it's taken me a while to get the hang of the techy side of running a business but Canva makes creating so easy.
Start by having a play and personalising some templates that are already created for you. Search for a template you would like, e.g. Insta post and then choose one. From there you can change the colours, the font, effects, add your logo, etc, so many options. It's really easy. Go have a play!

### What or who in the world inspires you?
Lots of things and people inspire me but my main inspiration is myself, lol, I know I can do anything I put my mind to and we already have inside us everything we need.
My partner, Paul, he is such a kind, thoughtful and caring person and I know he has my back 100% and for that I am so grateful, he means the world to me and even when I feel like giving up, he helps me keep going! Natasha Bray, one incredible lady, such an inspiration. I have followed her journey from minimum wage to millionaire and I know ANYTHING is possible because of her. I am worthy and I am capable! Check her out @natashabray on FB & Insta.

### How did you create this piece?
I created this piece on Canva because my message is to motivate, inspire and empower you to live your best life so I wanted to share one of my favourite quotes with you all. I created this piece by creating the background with raindrops, in the background effects using the gradient options and scrolled through and chose the one I wanted. For the image in the centre, I wanted it to not be square or a regular circle so I went through the shape upload area and chose the "sun/flower" shape, I wanted to add the image to that shape only. I wanted to have a rainbow that really stood out, so searched for one in the photos section on Canva Pro. Then I chose the image I wanted. Because I wanted the rainbow and colours to stand out more, I went into photo effects option, while clicking on the image so it was only that image that changed and chose the effect I wanted. Lastly I needed to add the quote, so I chose my favourite font and applied over the rainbow image and made the text bold and chose the colour white for the text as it stood out the most. I wanted to keep the image simple but hopefully effective.

### How can we contact you?

 @flawsomejem    @flawsomejem    www.flawsomejem.com

CREATIVE DESIGN PROJECT

# Alison Barnicott

**Name:**

Alison Barnicott

**Business:**

Administrative Virtual Assistant

### Who do you help with your business?

Other VA's or clients with the overwhelm of general administration and other tasks.

### What products or services do you offer?

All that is administration from HR, proofreading, KDP publishing, Email and diary management, live content typing, minute taking, Mailchimp campaigns and so much more.

### How long have you been using Canva and what do you create?

About a year and I love creating branded posts for my social media as well as for fun. I also want to use it to design my own greeting cards in the future.

### What advice would you offer someone just starting out?

Enjoy it and have a play around to start with. In time you will be able to create wonderful branding etc., with experience and you will be amazed what creations you can produce including animations and short reels.

### What or who in the world inspires you?

All the entrepreneurs on Dragons Den, I think they are amazing with their achievements and everything they offer to budding entrepreneurs.

---

### How did you create this piece?

Totally from scratch using elements and by moving them to the back and front of the picture accordingly.

### How can we contact you?

 @booksandbobsab

 booksandbobsab@gmail.com

CREATIVE DESIGN PROJECT

**Paulene Burton**

**Name:**

Paulene Burton

**Business:**

P Kuumba Designs

## Who do you help with your business?

I help design and create digital art for creatives who are not able to create designs for themselves or to save time for them. I help with creating tutorials to help explain how to create designs for Print on Demand (POD) e.g. Cushions, Mugs, Journals for KDP, Lulu, Cards etc.

## What products or services do you offer?

I offer digital products e.g. digital art, digital dolls, digital paper, printables. Physical products for POD e.g. mugs, journals, notebooks, planners, cushions, blankets, cards, tote-bags, t-shirts, travel and home apparel, bookmarks, colouring books, SVG's, PNG's and PDF's, I also offer personalised designs for journals and home and travel apparel etc... Classes relating to POD.

## How long have you been using Canva and what do you create?

I have been aware of Canva since 2017 but have been actively using it since 2019.
I can create many things e.g. digital and physical products – digital art, digital graphics, illustrations digital paper, surface pattern designs, social media post backgrounds, printables, journal/planner covers, stickers, templates, posters, vision boards, various plans, calendars, tutorials, colouring pages, journals/notebooks, svg's, animations.

## What advice would you offer someone just starting out?

I would advise them to have a go with Canva. There is so much available in Canva to create and design many things. Make use of the templates to give them a headstart if they are not sure what to do. Take classes to increase your knowledge and skills to use Canva. The drag and drop feature is very useful.

## What or who in the world inspires you?

Usually anything inspires me and then I may create something relating to it i.e. the ocean, dolphins (my favourite sea animal) prints & sea shells, textiles, crafts, sewing, graphic design, technology, art galleries and museums. My faith, abstract designs, lions, eagles, flowers, bright colours, fashion designers. plants, architectural designs. Michelle Obama, Pucci, CoCo, Chanel.

---

## How did you create this piece?

Elements: – Woman Hairstyle, Descending Stripe Frame, Circle/Oval and Square Shapes, Gold Glitter Texture Background

## How can we contact you?

 @pkuumbadesigns   @pkuumbadesigns   www.linktree.com/pkuumbadesigns

CREATIVE DESIGN PROJECT

**Lauren Ward**

**Name:**

Lauren Ward

**Business:**

Where all the Books Live

### Who do you help with your business?

I support parents and grandparents with their children's interest in books to encourage reading for pleasure.

### What products or services do you offer?

I have a bookshop full of books for children and young people from an amazing array of authors. I create activity packs matched with books, childrens interest or themes.

### How long have you been using Canva and what do you create?

I have used Canva now for around sixteen months, I started to use it over Christmas in 2020. I create graphics for my social media posts, and I also use it to design activity sheets for the packs I create.

### What advice would you offer someone just starting out?

Don't be scared, just have a go and play around with it. The more you use it the more familiar you will become with it and the more fun you will have.

### What or who in the world inspires you?

Children inspire me, the wonder and awe they have of the world is something so special and magical.

### How did you create this piece?

I had an idea that I wanted to create a picture of a beautiful sunny day having fun in the park. I wanted to create an image that could be used in a story book or as a prompt to create a short story from.
I started off with the background choosing elements to create the sky, I layered different shapes adjusting the colours and transparency. I wanted to add a mountain to give different depths to the picture, I then looked for paths and bushes that I liked the shape and texture of, the trees I had seen previously and liked the look of them. I added flowers in the grass by flipping and cropping an element, the pond is double layered and I thought the frog and bunnies looked cute.
The children came next. I tried different children in varying poses but all from the same element creator as I loved the look of the design. Then once I had chosen the children I added in more flowers, the butterflies to match the children and lastly the clouds, sunshine and birds in the sky.

### How can we contact you?

 @whereallthebookslive     @whereallthebookslive

 www.book-parties.scholastic.co.uk/shop/Where-all-the-Books-Live

CREATIVE DESIGN PROJECT

**Bernie Denley**

## Name:

Bernie Denley

## Business:

Secret Gift Boutique

## Who do you help with your business?

I help people who are looking for a gift with a personalised touch for family and friends. My moto is the "gift is in the giving" this was very apparent during lockdown when people wanted personalised gifts sent to their friends and loved ones.

## What products or services do you offer?

I offer bespoke personalised gifts, ranging from clothing for wedding parties, anniversary gifts, accessories and gifts just because.

## How long have you been using Canva and what do you create?

I have been using Canva since the first lockdown.

## What advice would you offer someone just starting out?

My advice to anyone starting out with Canva is to experiment and save their favourite elements and make a brand kit for social media, it makes designing for business so much easier.

## What or who in the world inspires you?

I am going to be honest, I had to think about this one for a while, as the word inspire carries a lot of weight. After contemplating this answer, I couldn't put my finger on who, but I could with what, and that is kindness, people who go out of their way to help the least fortunate or minorities.

## How did you create this piece?

I started with a blank template, I had been sitting outside in the nice warm weather and I was journaling/writing down goals and started to doodle a butterfly and wrote, "Life can flutterby" I have always loved butterflies, they are beautiful. I recently had spinal surgery and during my operation there was some complications and I flatlined a number of times, during my recovery I missed out on so much and decided that I was going to say yes to everything as "Life and Time" go by so quickly, I didn't want to miss out! Using Canva elements I was able to create something that I stand by and believe.

## How can we contact you?

 @secretgiftboutique    @bernie.denley

# Nikki Ince

**Name:**

Nikki Ince

**Business:**

Willow Social - Social Media Virtual Assistant and Canva Champion

## Who do you help with your business?

I help service-based small business owners and start-ups who know they need to be on social media but struggle with time and feel a bit overwhelmed with what they need to do and how.

## What products or services do you offer?

Social media support, scheduling content using Facebook Business Suite, social media graphics creation using Canva,
Social media content library creation and organising using Trello, Power Hours: Canva, Trello, Facebook, Facebook group community support.

## How long have you been using Canva and what do you create?

I started using Canva in 2015 creating Facebook page graphics. Since then, I have used Canva to create social media graphics for clients. I upgraded to Canva Pro during lockdown and have started creating templates and workbooks. I love trying out all the new features!

## What advice would you offer someone just starting out?

For someone starting their own business, find a local networking group or join Facebook groups to make connections and get tips and advice. No question is ever a silly question, and the right community will help and support you when needed.

## What or who in the world inspires you?

The last two years have been challenging for so many and I have been inspired by the volunteering, caring and support that brought people together in difficult circumstances. It was also inspiring to see small business owners adapting and changing how they worked to keep their businesses running.

---

## How did you create this piece?

This was created using Canva Pro, I used watercolour elements to create the background and searched keywords such as rainforest, forest, nature, monkeys, vines, and grass to build up the layers. This is not something I normally create on Canva, and it was fun to get creative in a totally different way. Monkeys are my favourite animal so that was my inspiration.

## How can we contact you?

 @thewillowsocial    @thewillowsocial    willowsocial.co.uk

# Amy Braybrook

## Name:

Amy Braybrook

## Business:

Miss A.M.I

## Who do you help with your business?

Anyone that is looking for a better way to organise their notes, or plan their work and family life. I help people that love stationary and I also help people that are looking for something unique, with personalised options for work or personal use.

## What products or services do you offer?

Notebooks, planners, trackers and books. Free support group for journaling. In person business meet up's and I am a fiction author.

## How long have you been using Canva and what do you create?

Roughly three to four years, I create visual aids for my business, as well as leaflets and business cards. I also use it for personal use such as birthday cards, posters etc.

## What advice would you offer someone just starting out?

Trust your gut, believe in yourself and make sure you surround yourself with good people. When you can, also look at outsourcing things you struggle to do or don't like doing and don't be scared of using a mentor.

## What or who in the world inspires you?

My daughter inspires me every day, not only to do my best but to also show her that anything is possible if you believe in yourself and put your mind to it.

---

## How did you create this piece?

I started by searching for a watercolour background, I knew I wanted a nature theme and so I then looked for animals and flowers I liked the look of, and positioned them so that they complimented each other and all fitted.

## How can we contact you?

 www.miss-ami.co.uk

 @MissAMIonline   @miss_a.m.i_online   @miss_a.m.i

CREATIVE DESIGN PROJECT

## Lucy Piper

### Name:

Lucy Piper (formerly known as Hutchinson)

### Business:

Director and owner of Any Little Thing Ltd

## Who do you help with your business?

We are a home help service for the elderly and vulnerable, my business partner and I absolutely love helping others. Our customers and those that are less fortunate than myself with their health, inspire me every day, we absolutely love what we do.

## What products or services do you offer?

We offer a range of home help services for the elderly and vulnerable including cleaning, household chores, appointment transport, companionship, prescription collection and delivery, dog walking and much more. Our job is to provide support for our customer and their family. Care companies cover their needs, we cover their wants. It truly is a pleasure!

## How long have you been using Canva and what do you create?

We use Canva for creating some of our marketing material but mainly to schedule our social media.

## What advice would you offer someone just starting out?

My advice would be to not over think and simply get creative and of course to ask for advice where needed. If you are not sure how to do something, there is always someone else that can help.

## What or who in the world inspires you?

I have worked in the care industry for some time now. I have to say that it is some of the many customers I have been lucky enough to work with that have inspired me along the way. No matter what their disabilities or their elderly age they either share their inspiring stories or enjoy every moment they live in. It is so easy to get dragged down with the issues we may come across in life or the difficulties we face, but we must remember that life is a gift and to be grateful and wonderous in this world is key.

---

## How did you create this piece?

I love butterflies, and I love bright colours. So much so, that they are incorporated into our company logo for Any Little Thing Ltd. I started with a background colour and design that incorporated in all these things. The beauty of Canva is that it gives you so many ideas and different texts to choose from. You can swap and change your design so easily too. It really is a fab programme to use. The text was written with what inspires me in mind. We all need to be reminded exactly how precious life is from time to time.

## How can we contact you?

 @anylittlethingltd

 www.anylittlething.co.uk

# Nicole Bateman

**Name:**

Nicole Bateman

**Business:**

A Box Full of Joy

## Who do you help with your business?

I help anxious teens who don't feel good enough, and children who struggle to communicate their feelings. I also equip parents with strategies to help their children become more resilient, confident, and calm.

## What products or services do you offer?

I offer physical resources such as a card pack for exam stress, emotions processing pads to help deal with overwhelm and worry, gift boxes for encouragement and books.
I run workshops online and in person for parents to equip them with practical ways to support their anxious children. I also offer 1:1 coaching for pre-teens/teens to help them build their resilience and raise their confidence and self-esteem.

## How long have you been using Canva and what do you create?

I have been using Canva for about two years. Before starting A Box Full of Joy I used it in my teaching to create worksheets and now I use it for creating social media posts and posters for my business.

## What advice would you offer someone just starting out?

I would say to just try it out and give it a go! Have a look at templates to start with and see what you can create with a little bit of editing. Then, when you start to feel more confident you can start from scratch. I love the 'style' option that gives you colour combinations and if you have pro you can put in your own brand colours which saves time.

## What or who in the world inspires you?

My Grandad's sure and certain hope of where he was heading, even when faced with death, inspired me as a child. My parents ongoing passion for helping those on the fringes of society find hope and a way forward inspires me today.

## How did you create this piece?

I started with the theme of a 'glimmer of hope' in the darkness. I built up from the word hope by adding some sparkle and used the watercolour elements to depict the darkness. I added the drawn hands element on top of the watercolour to represent the fact that we are not alone.

## How can we contact you?

 @a.box.full.of.joy.uk    @a.box.full.of.joy.uk    www.aboxfullofjoyuk.co.uk

CREATIVE DESIGN PROJECT

# Natasha Williams

## Name:

Natasha Williams

## Business:

Betty's Bespoke Buys

## Who do you help with your business?

Mums and Small Business Owners

## What products or services do you offer?

As the proud owner of Betty's Bespoke Buys I offer a wide variety of products and services such as... personalised wall art prints, bespoke business stationary including logo designs. I also love to create custom cake toppers, various vinyl craft items and seasonal treats.

## How long have you been using Canva and what do you create?

I have been using Canva for over five years I use Canva to help me in all aspects of my business. This could be anything from designing the ideas of products I want to create, to making the products themselves to fulfil orders. I also enjoy using Canva to create all of the promotional graphics that I use to advertise my business over a range of social media platforms. It's so handy having all of the correct template sizes I need in one place, making content planning much easier and improving my consistency.

## What advice would you offer someone just starting out?

Don't be afraid to play around with the various elements Canva has to offer. I would highly recommend if you're a small business owner, like myself, to create your logo within Canva. Once you have done this you can then save the colours used as your branding kit. This is a great feature that Canva offers because you can then easily tweak the pre-designed templates to suit your own brand, this made my life much easier and saves me lots of time creating my content.

## What or who in the world inspires you?

The only person I rely on for inspiration is my four year old autistic son named Connor. Every day he wakes up with a smile on his face. Despite him being non verbal he doesn't let that hold him back from doing anything that he loves and enjoys to do, I myself have always loved digital design and anything crafts related, but I've never had the confidence to push myself to get it to where I want it to be. I want to be more than just a mum. If my son can overcome his own struggles then so can I. Whenever I look at him, he reminds me of why I'm doing what I love to do... so that my dreams of our future will one day come true.

## How did you create this piece?

I created this piece based around one of my favourite quotes... "Follow your dreams they know the way" this design is made up of lots of different graphic elements I found within Canva. To create this design it required a lot of layering of various individual elements, shapes and creating depth with colour. The design is of two girls who are on the journey to following their dreams no matter which path it takes them.

## How can we contact you?

 @bettys_bespoke_buys

 @BettysBespokeBuys123

 @bettys_bespoke_buys

CREATIVE DESIGN PROJECT

# Jas Virdee

46                             CREATIVE DESIGN PROJECT

**Name:**

Jas Virdee

**Business:**

Damson Design Studio

## Who do you help with your business?

Anyone that requires a design, whether that be social media posts, invitations, tickets, flyers or posters etc.

## What products or services do you offer?

My passion is to create, whether that be through the medium of photography or design, often a combination of both.
I create wall art and posters using my photography and digital designs.
I also offer design services for posters, invitations, tickets, flyers and social media pages.

## How long have you been using Canva and what do you create?

I've been using Canva for over a year and a half. Over this time I have created art posters, templates, book covers, invitations, a flyer and an album cover.
I also enjoy using my own photographs and adding elements or text in Canva.

## What advice would you offer someone just starting out?

Enjoy the process, spend time learning, playing and creating your style.
Make time every day to work on what you want to achieve, believe in yourself and those small steps forward soon add up

## What or who in the world inspires you?

Nature inspires me, my first love is nature/flower photography. Digital design has become another passion of mine, if I can combine the two then it's the best of both worlds!

---

## How did you create this piece?

It started with one single flower element, which was duplicated and double layered to create more petals. The design has then been built using many layers of splash and splatter elements around the edges of the flower to create a dissolved/dispersed effect. The splashes and splatters have been overlaid again and again, using only two colours (the colour of the flower and the colour of the background) crackle elements have been added to the edges to create texture.

## How can we contact you?

 jas@damsondesignstudio.co.uk       07360 141 936

# Emma Cole

**Name:**

Emma Cole

**Business:**

Emma Cole Photography

## Who do you help with your business?

I help women in business to become more visible and confident showing up online with beautiful personal branding photography. My photography experience helps to show their personality, brand ethos, energy and passion, which is magnetic to their dream clients.

## What products or services do you offer?

Personal branding photography
Headshot photography
Family photography
Training (creating the perfect brand)

## How long have you been using Canva and what do you create?

I have been using Canva Pro for a couple of years now for my business and love how quick and easy it is to create beautiful graphics. This is the first time I've created something for me that wasn't specifically for my business. Usually, I use Canva to create graphics for my social media posts, FB banners, PDFs for my training courses, blog covers, business cards etc. The things you can create with ease are endless!

## What advice would you offer someone just starting out?

Make carefully thought out investments for your business, don't go for everything because you think you should have it and don't waste loads of money on Facebook ads. Try and do it organically and show up... your face is your business so let them get to know you.

## What or who in the world inspires you?

Lisa Johnson for her integrity in business and drive to help business owners.
More importantly my little boy Noah, he is my Why and getting to spend more time with him and watch him grow up is the whole reason I started my business.

## How did you create this piece?

I usually use Canva for business purposes but this time I just let my creativity run wild and went back to my roots to create this watercolour piece. I specialised in watercolour during my illustration degree so I loved creating this without the mess. I started with a watercolour background for the water and added clouds, then I added watercolour elements like the tree line and mountains in the background to create dimension. Then built up the foreground keeping a careful eye on the colours I was using, to finish it off I created the detail elements using similar watercolour pieces from the same or similar artists.

## How can we contact you?

 www.emmacolephotography.co.uk

 @emmacolephotography   @emmacolephotographyofficial

# Animation

Try adding some animation to your graphics, did you know you can now animate the whole design or each element separately?

Add a bounce animation to your text and it gives your design that extra edge, or have an element scroll across the screen. When something moves, our eye is drawn to it, this is one of the reasons why social media platforms favour videos these days.

# Text Effects

Adding in text effects will help your information stand out, these are found in the effects section and include; shadow, hollow, neon, splice, glitch, echo, lift and a new one called background, where it adds a coloured background around the shape of the text itself. Using these can help bring the most important information forward on your design.

# Background Remover

If you have Canva PRO you have a background remover tool which is fantastic for images that have a messy background as you can take it out and add in your own. If you don't have pro you can use www.remove.bg a website that removes backgrounds on images for free, and then upload your image to Canva. You also have two additional tools to erase and restore to help with the little bits the remover tool misses or removes in error.

# Elements

Have a good look through the elements in Canva, type in any word that you would like to search for and you will have something come up. There are hundreds of thousands of elements in Canva and lots of them are animated, these are particularly good as motion captures our attention, so adding an animated element to your design will help. Every business owner in this book has used elements to create their artwork, and they are all different.

CREATIVE DESIGN PROJECT

# Your Brand Kit

Get your brand kit set up, my number 1 top tip. This will help make your life so much easier when it comes to creating templates and designs in Canva and if you have more than one business you can now create separate brand boards and toggle between them when designing!
You can either use the PRO Brand Kit or create yourself a brand board using a template on FREE.

## Keeping it simple

Keeping your designs simple and clear of clutter is key to visibility, don't be afraid of empty space in your designs, our brain loves organisation, and clear space is a winner for us. It's very tempting to fill it with everything we want to get across, so instead of everything in one design, try separating the information over multiple designs, giving you clean and clear graphics and more content for your socials.

## Grids & Frames

Make use of the Grids and Frames, these are great for quick easy graphics, that look effective, you can add in a grid, drop your images, add a bit of text and you have your social media graphic done. Type grid into the element section and you will find a lot of options, the great thing is you can add an image, a video or a colour to each individual block, meaning you can add a colour to any block then place your text over the top giving you space. Frames are awesome and really make a design stand out as you can have any shape, including letters, try creating a design with your name and then search for a pattern or gold image, drag it into the frame and you have a very effective design.

# Gradients & patterns for depth

Gradients or background patterns help to add depth to your design.

Adding a gradient or pattern to the background can make design stand out more, it stops it from looking flat. Use the transparency feature to soften your background pattern and this will help make your information, that you add on top, clearer and easier to read.

# Canva Keywords

Throughout the book you will find some keyword pages, these will include a small selection of the types of elements you will find when using these keywords, some classic, some fun and some very useful to know. Have fun discovering new elements.

### Gold Circle

### Gold star

### Gold background

### Gold frames

# Canva Keywords

All of the keywords in this book are available for both the free and PRO Canva accounts, so everyone has access to them.
Watercolour elements give your designs a softer, gentle look.

### Watercolour blobs

### Watercolour feathers

### Watercolour flowers

### Watercolour leaves

CREATIVE DESIGN PROJECT

# Canva Keywords

Pastel - Pastel icons and elements are quite popular on designs at the moment, check out a selection here. You can spend hours on Canva once you start finding elements you love as one always leads to another.

### Pastel icons

### Pastel backgrounds

### Pastel shapes

### Pastel - These have been created by @moonproject

60      CREATIVE DESIGN PROJECT

# Canva Keywords

**Sunburst Ray** - Here's a selection of elements you will get when searching Sunburst Ray, these are great for backgrounds or to help give your design a pop of colour.

CREATIVE DESIGN PROJECT

# Canva Keywords

**Neon Words** - These are great for brightening up a design, using them on promotional or sales posts works really well.

These are also all available through the FREE Canva account.

# Canva Keywords

**3D People** - A fun keyword for those who would like to use a face but you don't always want an image, these characters will give your graphics a pop of fun and colour, plus they are all available for FREE Canva users.

CREATIVE DESIGN PROJECT

# Canva Keywords

Letters - Here's a selection of letter elements, I couldn't miss these out, some of these are brilliant and most have the full alphabet available for you to use.

Type in the keyword, find the one you like then click the three dots ●●● and select "see more like this" for the full range.

### Tube Lamp

### Gold Letters

### Modern 3d Letters

### Isometric Letters

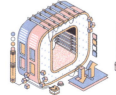

CREATIVE DESIGN PROJECT

# Canva Keywords

**Quote Decor** - I often find I like adding these types of elements around quotes, images and text, but can never really work out what they are called or what to search for. "Quote Decor"

# FEELING CREATIVE?

**Use this page to keep lists of keywords and design ideas you would like to try, there's also a few colouring pages for you to doodle on.**

**My favourite keywords to try**

**Design inspiration**

**Templates I love**

**68**  CREATIVE DESIGN PROJECT

# FEELING CREATIVE?

**My favourite keywords to try**

**Design inspiration**

**Templates I love**

**Notes**

CREATIVE DESIGN PROJECT

# FEELING CREATIVE?

**My favourite keywords to try**

**Design inspiration**

**Templates I love**

**Notes**

CREATIVE DESIGN PROJECT

# FEELING CREATIVE?

**My favourite keywords to try**

**Design inspiration**

**Templates I love**

**Notes**

# FEELING CREATIVE?

**My favourite keywords to try**

**Design inspiration**

**Templates I love**

**Notes**

# Businesses

Let's take a moment to celebrate and recognise the amazing businesses that have contributed to this book

Anna Rump - Amelia Rose Media Ltd

Stephanie Wium - Simply On Demand

Paula Garrard - By Paula Photography

Tracey Richardson - Hybrid Therapy

Sharon Barry - Little Gem Virtual Business Services

Mina Ahmed - Psychotherapist

Jessica Weeks - Hannah's House

Naomi Jane Johnson - Digital Content Designer

Joanna Cates - The Visual Storyteller, Joanna Cates Creates.

Laura Goodsell - Canva Coach and Digital designer at The Business Design Academy

Natalie McCoy - Urban Soul Holistic Therapy

Jemma Stevens - Flawsome Jem, CBD Products, Education & Support

Alison Barnicott - Administrative Virtual Assistant

Amy Breybrook - Miss A.M.I

Jillian Horan - Skincare consultant and a Virtual Assistant to beauty based and small retail businesses

Emma Cole - Emma Cole Photography

Nikki Ince - Willow Social – Social Media Virtual Assistant and Canva Champion

Lauren Ward - Where all the Books Live

Bernie Denley - Secret Gift Boutique

Pauline Burton-Gayle - P Kuumba Designs

Jas Virdee - Damson Design Studio

Natasha Williams - Betty's Bespoke Buys

Nicole Bateman -A Box Full of Joy

Lucy Piper - Director and owner of Any Little Thing Ltd

CREATIVE DESIGN PROJECT

# THANK YOU

If you would like to find out more about me and what I do, please check out my website www.businessdesignacademy.co.uk or come say hello on any of my Socials all under @createoncanva or
YouTube @createoncanvawithlaura

*Laura x*

Printed in Great Britain
by Amazon

84685635R00049